W9-BLV-414

12 BUSINESS LEADERS
WHO CHANGED THE WORLD

by Matthew McCabe

12 STORY LIBRARY

www.12StoryLibrary.com

12-Story Library is an imprint of Peterson Publishing Company and Press Room Editions.

Produced for 12-Story Library by Red Line Editorial

Photographs ©: Jeff Chiu/AP Images, cover, 1, 26; Nati Harnik/AP Images, 4; Najlah Feanny/Corbis, 5; Hulton-Deutsch Collection/Corbis, 6; pcruiciatti/Shutterstock Images, 7; Bettmann/Corbis, 8, 10; Everett Historical/Shutterstock Images, 9; s_bukley/Shutterstock Images, 11, 28; Hartsook/Library of Congress, 12; Library of Congress, 13, 23; Elaine Thompson/AP Images, 14; Aftab Alam Siddiqui/AP Images, 15; Ruth Fremson/AP Images, 16, 29; Kimberly White/Corbis, 18; Hadrian/Shutterstock Images, 19; Lawrence P. Ames/ Library of Congress, 20; Potomac Litho. Mfg. Co./Library of Congress, 21; Igor Golovniov/ Shutterstock Images, 22; Louie Psihoyos/Corbis, 24; Ken Wolter/Shutterstock Images, 25; Manoocher Deghati/AP Images, 27

ISBN
978-1-63235-145-6 (hardcover)
978-1-63235-186-9 (paperback)
978-1-62143-238-8 (hosted ebook)

Library of Congress Control Number: 2015934286

Printed in the United States of America
Mankato, MN
May, 2016

12
STORY
LIBRARY

Go beyond the book. Get free, up-to-date content on this topic at 12StoryLibrary.com.

TABLE OF CONTENTS

WARREN BUFFETT INVESTS IN THE LONG TERM

Warren Buffett is one of the world's richest people. He has made billions investing in the stock market. Buffett understands that investing is a long-term strategy. He also understands the role of value when investing. His investing strategy has changed the world.

Buffett made his first investment in 1942. He invested $120 in shares of Cities Service Preferred at the age of 11. It was all the money he had at the time. But by June of that year, he lost nearly all his money. Other people would have sold their shares and quit.

Buffett made billions by investing in the stock market.

BILLIONAIRES WORKING TOGETHER

Buffett has donated approximately $37 billion to the Bill and Melinda Gates Foundation. His donation is the largest in the history of the United States. But Buffett has not stopped there. He still donates approximately $2 billion each year to the foundation.

Buffett announces his large donation to the Bill and Melinda Gates Foundation in 2006.

But Buffett held on to his shares. He was patient. He knew that in time, the value of his shares would go up. He eventually sold his shares for a small profit. Buffett studied investing in college. After graduating, he got a job at a New York investment firm. He was successful finding stocks selling for less than they were worth. After a few years, Buffett started his own company in 1956. He became a millionaire in just six years. Today, he is worth approximately $73 billion.

Buffett donates much of his fortune to charity. He lives modestly. Buffett works with the Bill and Melinda Gates Foundation to help others. His wish is to give away his money while he is still alive. He wants to see his wealth help others.

Buffett has seen many investing trends come and go. But he has always invested in companies with value. This strategy has changed the investment world.

7

Decades during which Buffett perfected his value-based investing approach.

- Buffett believes the value of an investment is more important than its price.
- His strategy is to invest for the long term.
- Buffett donates much of his personal wealth to charity.

COCO CHANEL CHANGES THE CONCEPT OF BEAUTY

Coco Chanel changed the course of women's fashion. Her fashion designs introduced women to a wide range of clothing. Chanel changed the way women dressed and redefined beauty.

Chanel opened her first clothing shop in Paris in 1910. Her clothing designs were popular. But Chanel herself became a style icon. In the 1920s, women were expected to wear dresses or long skirts. It was not acceptable for women to wear pants. But then Chanel appeared in a pair of white pants at the beach. She believed pants should not be off-limits for women. Soon, other women started wearing pants. Chanel had given women more choice in the type of clothing they wore.

By accident, she also changed the meaning of beauty. In the early twentieth century, women wanted to have pale skin. Suntanned skin was

Chanel's fashion designs gave women the freedom to wear whatever they wanted.

6

identified with working outdoors. Then Chanel got a sunburn while on a cruise in 1923. When she returned to work, Chanel's tanned skin was admired by others.

However, Chanel No. 5 was her greatest achievement. Before Chanel No. 5, perfumes smelled like the flowers used to make them. Chanel created a perfume that included other ingredients. Chanel No. 5 was extremely popular when it went on sale in 1921. Today, it remains one of the most popular perfumes.

The Chanel Company continues to be a trendsetter.

CHANEL

FASHION THROUGH THE DECADES

Chanel opened her first shop in 1910. She influenced women's fashion in the 1920s. She continued to be a fashion leader until her death in 1971. Today, her company continues her legacy. The company still sells clothing and perfumes. It also sells makeup, jewelry, handbags, and watches.

80
Number of ingredients in Chanel No. 5.

- Chanel influenced the course of women's fashion.
- She helped make it okay for women to wear clothing other than skirts and dresses.
- The Chanel Company was the first to sell a perfume made of many different ingredients.

7

W. EDWARDS DEMING REBUILDS JAPAN'S ECONOMY

Good ideas can change the world. W. Edwards Deming was a business management expert in the 1950s. His ideas on product design helped improve companies and economies.

Deming studied mathematics in school. He used statistics to learn how good a company's products were. He also used statistics to discover how well a company was run. Deming believed good products came from driven workers with good tools. Before Deming, companies often blamed workers for bad products. But Deming believed poor management was to blame.

Deming put importance on doing a job right the first time. This idea changed how many industries created products. At first, many US companies ignored Deming. But Japanese companies asked for his help. Japan's economy was struggling after World War II (1939–1945). The war had been costly. Business leaders there wanted to make better

Deming believed good management was the key to business success.

Japan needed a lot of help rebuilding its economy after World War II.

products. People all over the world would buy good-quality products. In 1950, Deming visited with Japanese business leaders. Their companies started following Deming's advice. They improved how they operated. Soon, they were creating better products.

Deming's guidance turned Japan into one of the largest economies in the world. Companies such as Toyota and Sony succeeded thanks to Deming. Today, both are highly successful companies with good-quality products.

5
Number of American companies that sought Deming's advice.

- Deming used statistics to learn how successful a company was.
- He believed good products were result of smart employees with the right tools.
- Deming helped rebuild Japan's economy after World War II.

THINK ABOUT IT

Deming's advice helped Japanese companies attract American consumers. Many people bought Japanese products more than American products. Should US companies have paid more attention to his concepts?

4

WALT DISNEY'S ANIMATED FILMS ENCHANT CHILDREN

Children everywhere know Walt Disney's characters. Millions have grown up watching Mickey Mouse. Many families have visited Walt Disney World. Disney created films and shows for kids. His work changed the course of film history.

Disney began his work when movies were a new technology. Most films in the 1920s were for adults. Disney wanted to create a magical world for children to enjoy. Mickey Mouse was one of the first characters Disney created for children.

The Walt Disney Company created animated films. It was not the first company to do so. But Disney was the first to give its animated characters personalities. The company produced the first full-length animated film, *Snow White and the Seven Dwarfs*, in 1937. Some people thought a long animated movie would not be successful. But audiences loved *Snow White*. Today, the film is a classic. In 2008, the American Film Institute named it the Greatest Animated Film of All Time.

Disney produced some of the first films for children.

Today, the Disney Company runs theme parks where visitors can meet their favorite characters.

Walt Disney's films were the first to use new film technology. He used new camera technology to give the scenes in *Snow White* a more lifelike feel. In *Mary Poppins*, he mixed real people with animated characters.

54

Number of full-length animated films Disney produced between 1937 and 2014.

- Walt Disney created characters with personalities for children.
- He used new technology to improve his films.
- The Disney Company now creates films and owns TV channels and theme parks.

Walt Disney's work did not end with film. He created the Disneyland theme park in 1955. Disney wanted the park to educate and entertain visitors. *The Mickey Mouse Club* was a television series for children. Today, the Disney Company owns the ESPN and ABC TV channels. It has expanded from a small film studio to a company recognized the world over.

HENRY FORD CHANGES HOW PEOPLE GET AROUND TOWN

Henry Ford did not invent the car. He did not even create the first popular car. But he did change the way cars were made. His new manufacturing process changed the world. It also created the modern workday.

Before Ford, cars were expensive and often broke down. Ford believed cars should be affordable. He also thought they should be reliable. His solution to both problems was the assembly line. Ford broke the process of building a car into separate parts. Conveyor belts brought parts of a car from one station to the next. Workers stayed at the same station all day. They did not move around the factory floor. The system created a continuous, moving chain that sped up production.

Assembly lines quickly built cars the same way each time. Car prices fell, and their reliability increased. The Model T was Ford's first popular car. Before the assembly line, a Model T cost approximately $850. After Ford

Ford invented a system to make cars more reliable and affordable.

started using the assembly line in 1908, a Model T cost $360.

Ford also created the modern US workday. Before Ford, millions of Americans worked long days for low pay. Ford started paying his workers $5 for an eight-hour workday. In 2015, that would have been nearly $125 per day. The program also shortened the workweek from six days to five. This doubled the pay of his employees and allowed them

This assembly line in a Ford plant in Long Beach, California, is assembling car hoods.

to work fewer hours. The five-day workweek is still common today.

735,000

Number of Model Ts produced in a single year after the introduction of the assembly line.

- Ford wanted affordable, reliable cars for all Americans.
- He developed the concept of assembly lines.
- Ford made cars available to more people for less money.

FORD'S ASSEMBLY LINE

Henry Ford's assembly line changed more than the auto industry. Soon, other companies started using assembly lines. This made these other goods more affordable. People could save more money by spending less. They had the money to buy things they wanted, not just what they needed. His concept improved the lives of all Americans.

BILL GATES MAKES COMPUTERS EASY TO USE

New technologies rapidly change the world. Most Americans have computers in their homes. Bill Gates helped make the personal computer something anyone could buy and use. He and business partner Paul Allen founded Microsoft Corporation in 1975. Gates wanted to "put a computer on every desk in every home."

Other people were also developing computers. But Gates brought the technology into people's homes. Early computers were hard to use. Gates and

Microsoft developed the Windows operating system in 1985. Windows made it easier for people to use computers. People no longer needed to know computer code to operate one. Instead, Windows users could run their computers through different screens at the click of a mouse. Today, more than 90 percent of the world's personal computers run on Microsoft Windows.

Windows was not the only way Gates made computing easier for users. Microsoft Office made it simple to create electronic documents and other files. Office is still used in schools, offices, and homes around the world.

Gates's work at Microsoft has made him a successful businessman. He has a personal wealth of $60 billion. But he does not keep all his money. He has given away

Gates speaks at a meeting at Microsoft in 2013.

Melinda and Bill Gates at work in India in 2011

$26 billion in grants through the Bill and Melinda Gates Foundation. His philanthropy has supported food charities around the world. His donations have helped improve health in developing countries.

THE BILL AND MELINDA GATES FOUNDATION

Bill Gates and his wife, Melinda, have committed to donating 95 percent of their wealth. They do so through their charity, the Bill and Melinda Gates Foundation. The foundation has $42.3 billion to spend on different causes. The foundation provides funds to eliminate diseases such as HIV/AIDs and polio. It also provides money for health care for children.

15

Years Bill Gates has ranked as the richest person in the world by *Forbes* magazine, as of 2015.

- Gates made computers easy for anyone to use.
- His company created Microsoft Windows and Microsoft Office, programs used in millions of computers.
- Gates has committed to donating 95 percent of his fortune to charity.

KATHARINE GRAHAM LEADS A NATIONAL NEWSPAPER

Katharine Graham was once one of most powerful people in the United States. She owned the *Washington Post* newspaper from 1963 to 1979. She became the first woman to lead one of the top 500 most successful US companies. Under her direction, the *Post* covered two major political scandals. Her leadership helped give the paper a national reputation.

Graham's success came later in life. She was 46 when she took over the newspaper. Graham's father was wealthy New York banker Eugene Meyer. He purchased the *Washington Post* when Graham was 16. She worked at the paper in her youth. When she got married, her husband became president of the newspaper. Following his death, she took charge of the company.

The *Washington Post* company included the newspaper, *Newsweek* magazine, and two television

Graham led the *Washington Post* when it covered two major government scandals.

28

Years Graham led the *Washington Post*.

- Graham was the first woman to run a major US business.
- She oversaw reporting on the Pentagon Papers and the Watergate scandal.
- Under Graham's leadership, the *Washington Post* became one of America's finest newspapers.

THINK ABOUT IT

Graham had to make difficult decisions about the Pentagon Papers and Watergate. She had to decide whether or not to print the stories about wrongdoing in the government. Do you think she was right to publish the stories? Why or why not?

stations. Graham made sure the company's journalism was honest and fair. Under her guidance, the *Post* became one of the most respected newspapers in America. It published the Pentagon Papers in 1971. The documents revealed secret government actions during the Vietnam War (1955–1975). The information angered the public. The US government tried to stop the *Post* from reporting on the Pentagon Papers. Under Graham's leadership, the paper successfully fought the government in court.

Graham also supported her reporters during the Watergate scandal. She insisted the *Post* publish details of a break-in at the Watergate Hotel in 1972. The paper revealed wrongdoing by President Richard Nixon in the 1972 election. President Nixon eventually resigned because of the *Post*'s reporting.

STEVE JOBS HELPS DEVELOP THE IPHONE

Cell phones did not always have bright touchscreens. But many do today thanks to Steve Jobs. Jobs is the man responsible for making smartphones and tablets popular. He helped change the role cell phones play in society. As CEO, Jobs helped the Apple computer company become a global technology firm.

Jobs believed technology should also be art. In the 1980s, Apple designed computers for home use. Apple computers were easy to use. Jobs made sure they were well designed, too. In the 2000s, Apple started to work on a cell phone. At the time,

THINK ABOUT IT

People listen to music, check email, and share photos with iPhones and iPads. They use the devices to send messages to their friends and family. Some experts say people spend too much time on their phones and tablets. Do you agree or disagree? Why or why not?

Jobs introduces the iPad at a meeting in San Francisco, California, in 2010.

cell phones were simply functional. Some could get email, but most just made phone calls. Then, Apple released the iPhone in 2007. Cell phones became computers that could fit in a pocket.

The iPhone was the first touchscreen phone. It did not have a keyboard. It only had a few physical buttons. The design reflected Jobs's belief about technology as art. He wanted products that performed well and looked good, too. The iPhone was just one of Jobs's achievements. He and Apple popularized the tablet computer with the iPad. The iPad worked like a computer. But it could be carried around like a cell phone. Like the iPhone, the iPad had a touchscreen.

Jobs's ideas helped connect people all over the world. He helped change the way people communicate with each other. He helped show the world technology could be well designed, too.

169.22 million
Number of iPhones sold worldwide in 2014 alone.

- Jobs believed a piece of technology should also be art.
- Jobs changed the way people use cell phones.
- His company Apple created iPads and iPhones.

JOHN D. ROCKEFELLER FOUNDS STANDARD OIL

Oil and gas are essential fuels around the world. In the 1870s, US businessman John D. Rockefeller changed the way oil and gas were collected and processed.

Before Rockefeller, oil and gas were expensive fuels. He made oil and gas affordable for average Americans.

In the late nineteenth century, companies let much of the oil they drilled go to waste. Rockefeller developed a new business model to improve the industry. He founded Standard Oil Company in 1870. Standard Oil provided the best oil at the lowest price. Rockefeller grew his business by investing the money Standard Oil made back into the company. These business strategies changed the world.

Rockefeller's new ideas made Standard Oil a success. But it had many competitors. Standard Oil began to buy up these other

Rockefeller developed a way to make oil affordable for everyone.

companies. In 1882, Rockefeller and his business partners created the Standard Oil Trust. This large corporation eventually controlled 90 percent of US oil production. In 1911, the US Supreme Court ruled Standard Oil's control of the oil industry was illegal. The company was broken up into dozens of smaller companies. Many of them are still in business today. They include ExxonMobil, ConocoPhillips, and Chevron.

The American Red Cross received the Rockefeller Foundation's first donation.

34

Number of smaller companies created out of Standard Oil Trust.

- He developed ways to reduce the amount of oil wasted by the oil industry.
- Rockefeller grew Standard Oil by investing the money the business made back into the company.
- He donated some of his fortune to those in need.

ROCKEFELLER THE PHILANTHROPIST

Rockefeller donated money throughout his life. As a teenager, he gave 10 percent of his income to his church. As an adult, he believed rich people should use their money to help others. He formed the Rockefeller Foundation late in his life. The foundation donates money to worthy groups. Its first donation helped create the American Red Cross. Today, the Rockefeller Foundation has donated a total of $14 billion to various groups.

10

MADAM CJ WALKER REINVENTS HAIR CARE

Madam CJ Walker was a female business leader and millionaire. Many women today claim those same titles. But Walker's achievement is especially impressive. She was born to freed slaves in 1867. She became the first African-American millionaire and first female US millionaire.

Walker began her career as a saleswoman for Annie Turnbo Malone. Malone's business offered hair-care products to black women. Malone employed black women to sell her products.

Walker experienced hair loss as an adult. She started experimenting to find a product that helped her. She came up with her own formulas for hair-care products. Her products were made specifically for African Americans. In 1905, Walker started

This stamp celebrates Walker as an important African-American businesswoman.

BLACK HERITAGE

32 USA

Madam C.J. Walker

1998

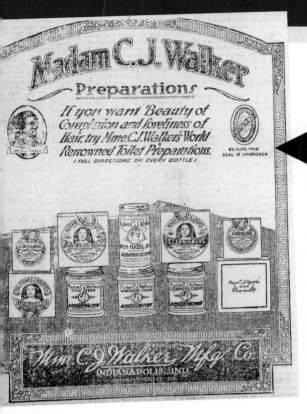

An early advertisement for Walker's products

Association for the Advancement of Colored People (NAACP). She also paid for young African Americans to go to the Tuskegee Institute. It is now called Tuskegee University.

her own company using these formulas. By 1910, she had started the Walker Company. It was one of the first to sell products solely to African Americans. Her business had a factory, training schools, and a number of salespeople selling her products. By 1919, her business was making $500,000 in sales each year. Before she died, Walker had become a millionaire.

Walker's hair-care products were very popular. But she was not just a businesswoman. She was also a philanthropist. She regularly donated money to the YMCA and National

9
Years it took Madam CJ Walker to earn her fortune.

- Walker was the first American woman to become a millionaire.
- She launched one of the first companies with products for African Americans.
- Walker used her fortune to help educate other African Americans.

23

SAM WALTON REVOLUTIONIZES RETAIL

Sam Walton founded Wal-Mart, the largest retail chain in the world. He believed stores should sell good products at low prices. He worked hard to provide the best prices possible. Today, there is at least one Wal-Mart in every state in the United States.

Walton thought retail stores should focus on their customers. As a young man, this idea got him into trouble. He was almost fired from his job at

JC Penney. He was excellent with customers but a bad record-keeper. Walton did not think service should suffer due to paperwork.

His career at JC Penney was interrupted by World War II. Walton served in the army until 1945. Afterward, he went into business for himself. The first store he opened was Walton's Five & Dime. His approach to retail was simple. He tried to price all his products below his competitors' prices. After 10 years in business, he owned 15 stores. But his retail system was not perfect. Walton's stores did not make enough money.

Walton began a new discounting strategy. It slashed prices below the competition. The stores made a profit by selling a greater number of

Walton opened his first store in the 1940s.

products. His strategy was unique in two other ways. First, he discounted every product his stores sold. Second, he built stores in small towns, not big cities.

Walton's approach was a success. People in rural areas were happy to shop for discounted products. In the 1970s, Wal-Marts started popping up across the country. Today, there are nearly 4,400 Wal-Marts in the United States. There are more than 6,200 Wal-Marts in other countries, too. The company provides 2.2 million jobs worldwide. Walton's strategy on how stores should sell products has changed retail across the world.

15

Number of stores Walton opened in Wal-Mart's first 10 years of doing business.

- Walton created a new retail strategy.
- He applied discount pricing to all the products his stores sold.
- Wal-Mart is now the world's largest retailer.

THINK ABOUT IT

Walton's vision required low prices and low costs. Wal-Mart keeps costs low by keeping wages low, too. Wal-Mart is criticized for paying workers low wages. How would increasing wages impact Walton's discounting strategy? Should Wal-Mart pay better wages?

MARK ZUCKERBERG CHANGES HOW PEOPLE COMMUNICATE

Facebook's founder Mark Zuckerberg wanted to make it easy for people to connect with friends. Today, the social media site has impacted the way companies do business. It has even helped people demand change from their government.

Zuckerberg launched Facebook in 2003 when he was just 19. He wanted to create a website for people to share thoughts and ideas. At first, Facebook was just for Harvard University students. Today, Facebook operates in 100 languages and 51 different countries. Facebook makes it easy for people to connect with others at home and around the world.

Facebook is no longer just for individuals. Businesses use it to build relationships with consumers. Companies can connect directly with customers. They share product photos and make special offers. Customers use Facebook to praise

By creating Facebook, Zuckerberg helped change the world.

1.39 billion

Number of active Facebook accounts worldwide in December 2014.

- Zuckerberg created Facebook when he was 19.
- He wanted to change the way people shared information.
- His company has impacted business, political, and personal relationships.

THINK ABOUT IT

Zuckerberg created Facebook to make communication easier. People do not need to call or see each other to remain friends. Friends "like" photos and share posts to maintain contact. Has Facebook altered friendship in a negative way? If yes, how so? If no, why not?

good service and complain about poor service.

In countries such as Egypt and Iran, the government limits information available to citizens. But Facebook allows people to share information instantly. People can use this information before the government can delete it. In 2011, people in Egypt organized an uprising, in part, on Facebook. The website created for Harvard students has changed the world.

An Egyptian art student paints "Facebook" on a mural that celebrates the 2011 protests in Egypt.

27

HOW YOU CAN MAKE CHANGE

Think Differently

Many business leaders changed the world by thinking up new solutions for common problems. Look around your school. Write a polite letter to your principal that includes a creative way to solve a problem or make something better. Ask your classmates if they would like to help you.

Work Hard

Facebook, Standard Oil, and the *Washington Post* were not made overnight. Their founders worked hard to make them successful. Think about your favorite things to do. How could working a little bit harder make you more successful? Make a plan to keep track of your progress.

Be Generous

Lots of business leaders donate money. But you do not have to be wealthy to give to charity. Organize a book drive to donate books to children in need. Ask an adult to volunteer with you at an animal shelter or soup kitchen.

GLOSSARY

assembly line
An arrangement of equipment and workers in which a product is put together piece by piece in a direct line until complete.

competitors
Companies that sell the same goods and services.

conveyor belts
Pieces of machinery that move parts and equipment from one place to another in a factory.

economies
The systems countries use to produce, sell, and buy goods and services.

industry
A group of businesses that create a particular good or service.

investing
Using money to purchase shares in a company in order to make money.

management
Act of controlling and making decisions about a business.

operating system
The main program that controls a computer.

philanthropy
Giving money and time to make life better for other people.

retail
Business of selling things directly to customers.

shares
Equal parts of a company that represent ownership in that company.

stock market
A system for buying and selling shares of a company.

FOR MORE INFORMATION

Books

Furtig, Dennis. *Mark Zuckerberg*. Chicago: Heinemann Library, 2013.

Matthews, Elizabeth. *Different Like Coco*. Cambridge, MA: Candlewick Press, 2007.

McKissack, Patricia, and Fredrick McKissack. *Madam C.J. Walker: Inventor and Millionaire*. Berkeley Heights, NJ: Enslow Publishers, 2013.

Websites

Be Your Own Boss Business Games
www.pbskids.org/itsmylife/games/boss

Five Tips for Teen Entrepreneurs
www.kidshealth.org/teen/school_jobs/jobs/tips_business.html

Managing Money: It's My Life Money Tips
www.pbskids.org/itsmylife/money/managing/article9.html

INDEX

About the Author

Matthew McCabe is a freelance writer
and resident of Plymouth, Minnesota.
He has worked as a writer for six
years, covering a variety of topics
ranging from sports and travel to
business technology.

READ MORE FROM 12-STORY LIBRARY

Every 12-Story Library book
is available in many formats,
including Amazon Kindle
and Apple iBooks. For more
information, visit your device's
store or 12StoryLibrary.com.